# main courses

# Rick Stein *main courses*

Published by BBC Books, BBC Worldwide Ltd,
Woodlands, 80 Wood Lane, London W12 0TT

First published 2004
Reprinted 2005
Copyright © Rick Stein 2004
The moral right of the author has been asserted

Food photography © James Murphy 1999, 2000,
2002 and 2004.
Location photography © Craig Easton 2000
Portrait of Rick Stein and Chalky on page 6
© David Pritchard 1999

The recipes in this book first appeared in the
following titles: **Fruits of the Sea**, **Seafood Odyssey**,
**Seafood Lovers' Guide**, **Seafood**, **Food Heroes** and
**Food Heroes: Another Helping**, which were
originally published by BBC Worldwide in 1997,
1999, 2000, 2001, 2002 and 2004 respectively.

ISBN 0 563 52190 2

Commissioning Editor: Vivien Bowler
Project Editors: Rachel Copus and Warren Albers
Designer: Andrew Barron
Production Controller: Kenneth McKay
Food Stylist: Debbie Major

Set in Din and Veljovic
Printed and bound in Italy by L.E.G.O SpA
Colour separations by Butler and Tanner Ltd

Jacket photography:
Food photography and portrait of Rick Stein
© James Murphy 2004
Landscape photography © Craig Easton 2000

# contents

There's a lot to read in most cookery books. Sometimes I think one is spoiled for choice. Guided by the theory that 'less is more', I thought that three books each containing a dozen or so recipes covering first courses, main courses and puddings would be a welcome alternative. So I've compiled three mini cookery books, choosing the recipes from the nine books I've written to give the widest possible range of dishes that best illustrate my personal style of cooking. I like to think of them as my 'best of' recipe collections.

To illustrate this, I joke with the producer of my TV series, David Pritchard, that most of his CD collection seems to be labelled 'The best of'. I call him Compilation Man, which hurts him a little because actually he has a very acute knowledge of music. But sometimes a slim volume of 'best of' dishes like this sets a boundary on cooking at a time when you might be suffering from information overload.

I have fanciful thoughts that these would be all you need, say, on holiday, cooking in a rented house or villa. You could slip these slim volumes into your luggage and be armed with a repertoire of enough dishes to deal with a light lunch over a glass of wine, supper for the children or a serious dinner for a party of friends.

Oddly enough, high up in my all-time favourite recipes is a dish that doesn't feature seafood. It's **Crisp Chinese roast pork**. I think this, and several other dishes in the first of my general cookbooks, **Food Heroes**, surprised people because not only was it not fish, but it wasn't British either. The point of that book, however, was to celebrate great British produce and in this case it was belly pork. As I pointed out in the TV series, the Chinese revere belly pork above all other cuts and this dish shows why. It never fails to please with its crisp, aromatic, crackling skin and meltingly tender meat, cut into cubes and served with steamed Chinese greens and boiled rice. I like to slip in a small dish of hot chilli sauce, like XO, when I'm serving it and would choose a New Zealand Pinot Noir above all other wines to accompany it.

I may be guilty, as the Australians say, of 'big-noting myself' but, looking through these recipes, I'm so enthused about how much I want to cook them. Take **Barbecued butterflied lamb**, for example. I remember writing in the introduction to that recipe, 'This is one of those recipes that I have to limit myself to cooking occasionally, otherwise I'd overdose on it, it's that good.' But not only is it good, it seems to be the sort of food that everyone else likes too: rough slices of pink lamb tinged with the flavour of the fire.

As with the other two mini cookery books, I've tried to be as wide-ranging as possible in my choice, so I've included an interesting vegetarian dish in **Leek cannelloni with lemon thyme.** At the time of creating it I was thinking that vegetarian food should be about recipes that don't happen to have meat or fish in them, rather than ones that have been specifically written for non-meat-eaters. I love the way the leeks melt in with the ricotta, and the combination of béchamel and tomato sauces with the final sprinkling of grated provolone cheese heated under a grill is superb.

Continuing my attempt to cover as many types of main course as possible, I've included a very traditional **Beef, Guinness and oyster pie.** When I first cooked this dark, full-flavoured pie in the restaurant during the mid-seventies, I have to confess I was a bit stingy with the oysters. We used to make it in individual brown earthenware dishes, and very popular it was too. Now that we can afford it a lot more oysters go into it, which gives it a beguiling creaminess and also the same sort of salty, savoury taste that anchovies give to a French daube or oyster sauce to a Chinese beef stir-fry.

Seafood dishes naturally feature largely and those included are all simple recipes that can be cooked successfully at home or, as in the case of **Lobster thermidor,** restaurant dishes that you can cook at home without too much difficulty. **Seared escalopes of wild salmon** is a particular favourite because it is a very last-minute dish. It exemplifies, paradoxically, what I brought to my restaurant cooking – amateurishness. I wasn't aware of the tricks of the trade, which means largely precooking everything to make it easier to serve. I just assumed everyone did things at the last minute. Incidentally, since writing this recipe, I've discovered that adding a tablespoonful of very well-reduced red wine to the caramelised vinegar will improve the depth of the sauce no end. To do this you need to cook down about half a bottle of red wine – perhaps left over from dinner – with a tablespoon of sugar to, literally, half a wine glassful.

The other seafood dishes are similarly great favourites, such as the **Prawn caldine**, a Goan seafood curry, which I always think is such an appropriate way to serve good warm-water prawns, and the **Roast monkfish with crushed potatoes**, one of those dishes that constantly appears on one of our menus but which is impossibly easy to make at home. Incidentally, I find the practice of not peeling small potatoes to suggest they are new quite off-putting, and for this dish, unless you can remove the skins by rubbing them with your thumb, some sort of scraping or peeling improves the flavour immensely.

# main courses

## grilled cod on spring onion mash

SERVES 4

**4 x 175–225 g (6–8 oz) pieces
of unskinned thick cod fillet
Salt and black pepper
A little melted butter,
for brushing**

FOR THE SPRING
ONION MASH
**1.25 kg (2½ lb) potatoes,
peeled and cut into chunks
50 g (2 oz) butter
1 bunch spring onions,
trimmed and thinly sliced
A little milk
Salt and ground white pepper**

FOR THE SOY
BUTTER SAUCE
**600 ml (1 pint) Chicken stock
(see page 38)
2 tablespoons dark soy sauce
75 g (3 oz) unsalted butter
1 tomato, skinned, seeded
and diced
1 heaped teaspoon
chopped coriander**

**1** Put the fish, skin-side down, in a shallow dish and sprinkle with 1 teaspoon of salt. Set aside for 30 minutes.

**2** Rinse the salt off the fish pieces and dry well. Brush them with melted butter and put skin-side up on a greased baking tray. Sprinkle with a little salt and some coarsely crushed black pepper.

**3** For the spring onion mash, cook the potatoes in boiling unsalted water for 20 minutes until tender.

**4** Meanwhile, for the sauce, put the stock and soy sauce into another pan and boil rapidly until reduced by half.

**5** Preheat the grill to high. Grill the cod for 8 minutes on one side only.

**6** Just before the fish is ready, add the butter to the sauce and whisk until blended. Remove from the heat and add the tomato and chopped coriander.

**7** Drain the potatoes, return them to the pan and mash until smooth. Heat the butter in another pan, add the spring onions and cook for a few seconds. Beat into the potato with a little milk, salt and white pepper. Spoon the mash into the centre of each plate. Rest the cod on top and spoon the sauce around the outside.

# lobster thermidor

**1 x 675 g (1½ lb)
cooked lobster
25 g (1 oz) butter
2 large shallots,
finely chopped
600 ml (1 pint) Fish stock
(see page 38)
50 ml (2 fl oz) dry white
vermouth, such as
Noilly Prat
85 ml (3 fl oz) double cream
½ teaspoon English mustard
1 teaspoon chopped mixed
fines herbes (chervil,
tarragon, parsley
and chives)
1 teaspoon lemon juice
15 g (½ oz) Parmesan cheese,
freshly grated
Salt and black pepper**

**1** To remove the meat from the lobster, twist off the claws and legs and discard the legs. Break the claws into pieces at the joints, crack the shells with a large knife and remove the meat from each section. Now cut the lobster in half lengthways – first through the middle of the head between the eyes, then turn it around and cut through the tail. Open it up and remove the meat from each half. Remove the dark intestinal tract and cut the meat into small, chunky pieces. Remove the soft, greenish tomalley and any red roe from the head section of the shell and set aside. Pull out the stomach sac (a slightly clear pouch) from the head section and discard. Transfer the cleaned half-shells to a baking sheet and evenly distribute the tail and claw meat between them with any red roe. Cover and set aside.

**2** For the sauce, melt the butter in a small pan, add the shallots and cook gently for 3–4 minutes, until soft but not browned. Add the fish stock, vermouth and half the double cream and boil until reduced by three-quarters. Add the rest of the cream and simmer until the sauce has reduced to a good coating consistency. Whisk in the reserved tomalley, the mustard, herbs, lemon juice and seasoning.

**3** Preheat the grill to high. Spoon the sauce over the lobster and sprinkle with the Parmesan cheese. Grill for 2–3 minutes, until golden and bubbling.

SERVES 6

**900 g (2 lb) braising steak,
such as blade or chuck,
cut into 4–5 cm
(1½–2 in) chunks
25 g (1 oz) plain flour
5 tablespoons sunflower oil
25 g (1 oz) unsalted butter
225 g (8 oz) small button
mushrooms, trimmed
2 onions, thinly sliced
½ teaspoon sugar
300 ml (10 fl oz) Guinness
300 ml (10 fl oz) Beef broth
(see page 39)
3 sprigs of thyme
2 bay leaves
2 tablespoons
Worcestershire sauce
12 Pacific oysters (optional)
500 g (1 lb) chilled puff pastry
A little beaten egg,
for brushing
Salt and freshly ground
black pepper**

**1** Season the steak, toss with the flour and shake off and reserve the excess. Heat 3 tablespoons of the oil in a large pan and brown the meat in batches until well coloured. Set aside.

**2** Add another tablespoon of the oil, half the butter and the mushrooms to the pan and fry briefly. Set aside. Add the rest of the oil and butter, the onions and sugar and fry over a medium-high heat for 20 minutes, until browned. Stir in the reserved flour, gradually add the Guinness and stock and bring to the boil. Return the beef and mushrooms to the pan with the herbs, Worcestershire sauce, ¾ teaspoon of salt and some pepper, cover and simmer for 1½ hours.

**3** Lift the meat, mushrooms and onions out of the liquid and put into a deep 1.75 litre (3 pint) pie dish. Rapidly boil the liquid until reduced to 600 ml (1 pint). Remove the bay leaves and thyme twigs and pour into the pie dish. Leave to cool.

**4** Preheat the oven to 200°C/400°F/Gas Mark 6. Open the oysters, if using (see page 43), add to the dish and push them down well into the sauce. Push a pie funnel into the centre.

**5** Roll out the pastry and use to cover the top of the pie dish, cutting a small cross in the centre for the pie funnel. Chill for 20 minutes.

**6** Brush the pie with egg and bake for 30–35 minutes.

# warm **roast chicken salad**

SERVES 4

**50 g (2 oz) butter, softened**
**1 tablespoon roughly**
**chopped tarragon**
**2 large garlic cloves, crushed**
**1 x 1.75 kg (4 lb)**
**free-range chicken**
**1 tablespoon sunflower oil**
**Salt and black pepper**

FOR THE DRESSING
**150 ml (5 fl oz) Mayonnaise**
**(see page 40)**
**1 teaspoon chopped tarragon**
**3 tablespoons single cream**
**½ teaspoon English mustard**
**1 teaspoon tarragon vinegar**

FOR THE SALAD
**Leaves from 2 soft lettuces**
**4 vine-ripened tomatoes,**
**cut into wedges**
**½ cucumber, peeled**
**and sliced**
**12 radishes, halved**
**12 spring onions, halved**
**4 large eggs**

**1** Preheat the oven to 200°C/400°F/Gas Mark 6. Mix together the butter, tarragon, garlic and some salt and pepper. Put the flavoured butter into the cavity of the chicken, then brush the outside of the bird with the oil and season with salt and pepper. Put into a small roasting tin and roast for 1¼ hours, basting the chicken with the buttery juices for the last 10 minutes of cooking.

**2** Meanwhile, prepare the salad. For the dressing, whisk all the ingredients together until smooth and then season to taste. Arrange the lettuce leaves over a large serving platter with the tomatoes, cucumber, radishes and spring onions. Cover and leave somewhere cool.

**3** Remove the chicken from the oven and leave to rest for about 15 minutes. Meanwhile, add the eggs to a pan of simmering water and boil for 8 minutes. Remove and set aside.

**4** To joint the chicken, cut the breast meat away from the bones in 2 whole pieces and then slice each piece in half on the diagonal. Cut off the legs and cut them in half at the joint. Shell the warm eggs and cut them into quarters.

**5** Arrange the warm chicken pieces and eggs over the salad and drizzle with a little of the dressing. Take to the table with a bowl of the remaining dressing.

# moussaka

SERVES 6

150–175 ml (5–6 fl oz)
olive oil
1 large onion, finely chopped
3 garlic cloves, crushed
900 g (2 lb) lean minced lamb
50 ml (2 fl oz) white wine
(a generous splash)
400 g (14 oz) can
chopped tomatoes
5 cm (2 in) piece
of cinnamon stick
A handful of fresh oregano
leaves, preferably wild
Greek oregano, chopped
3 large aubergines,
cut lengthways into slices
5 mm (¼ in) thick
Salt and black pepper

FOR THE TOPPING
75 g (3 oz) butter
75 g (3 oz) plain flour
600 ml (1 pint)
full-cream milk
50 g (2 oz) Parmesan cheese,
freshly grated
2 medium eggs, beaten

**1** Heat 2 tablespoons of the oil in a pan, add the onion and garlic and fry until just beginning to brown. Add the minced lamb and fry over a high heat for 3–4 minutes. Add the wine, tomatoes, cinnamon and oregano and simmer gently for 30–40 minutes while you prepare everything else.

**2** Heat a frying pan until it is very hot, add 1 tablespoon of the oil and a layer of aubergine slices and fry quickly until tender and lightly coloured on both sides. Lift out with tongs and arrange over the base of a deep 2.5–2.75 litre (4½–5 pint) ovenproof baking dish. Season lightly with a little salt and pepper. Repeat with the rest of the oil and the aubergines, seasoning each layer as you go.

**3** For the topping, melt the butter in a pan, add the flour and cook, stirring, over a medium heat for 1 minute. Gradually beat in the milk, then bring to the boil, stirring. Simmer very gently for 10 minutes, stirring occasionally. Add the cheese and some salt and pepper to taste. Cool slightly and then beat in the eggs.

**4** Preheat the oven to 200°C/400°F/Gas Mark 6. Remove the cinnamon stick from the lamb sauce, season to taste with some salt and pepper and spread it over the aubergines. Pour the topping over the sauce and bake for 25–30 minutes, until golden and bubbling.

# baked guinea fowl with garlic beans

SERVES 4

**225 g (8 oz) dried haricot beans, soaked in cold water overnight**
**1 tablespoon olive oil**
**1 x 1.5 kg (3 lb) guinea fowl**
**2 heads of garlic, broken into individual cloves and peeled**
**25 g (1 oz) butter**
**50 g (2 oz) smoked bacon lardons (short fat strips)**
**The leaves from a large sprig of rosemary**
**1 x 225 g (8 oz) smoked sausage, cut into chunky slices**
**150 ml (5 fl oz) Chicken stock (see page 38)**
**Salt and black pepper**

**1** Drain the beans, put them into a saucepan and cover with plenty of fresh cold water. Bring to the boil and simmer gently for 30 minutes–1 hour (this will depend on the age of your beans), until just tender, adding 1 teaspoon of salt 5 minutes before the end of cooking. Drain and set aside.

**2** Preheat the oven to 200°C/400°F/Gas Mark 6. Heat the olive oil in a medium-sized flameproof casserole. Season the guinea fowl, add it to the casserole and brown it on all sides. Turn the bird breast-side up and add the garlic cloves, butter, bacon lardons and rosemary to the casserole. Cover with a tight-fitting lid, transfer to the oven and cook for 30 minutes.

**3** Add the beans, smoked sausage, chicken stock, ½ teaspoon of salt and some black pepper to the casserole and stir once or twice to coat everything in the cooking juices. Continue to cook, covered, for a further 30 minutes or until the guinea fowl is tender and cooked through.

**4** To serve, lift the guinea fowl on to a board, cut off the legs and cut each one in half at the joint. Cut the breast meat away from the carcass in 2 whole pieces and slice on the diagonal. Divide the beans between 4 warmed, deep, bistro-style plates and place one piece of leg and some of the sliced breast meat on top.

SERVES 4

**550 g (1¼ lb) headless
raw prawns
2 tablespoons coconut vinegar
or white wine vinegar
1 teaspoon turmeric powder
1 teaspoon black peppercorns
1 tablespoon coriander seeds
1 teaspoon cumin seeds
2 tablespoons white poppy
seeds or ground almonds
4 tablespoons groundnut oil
1 onion, thinly sliced
3 garlic cloves, cut into slivers
2.5 cm (1 in) fresh
ginger, finely chopped
400 ml (14 fl oz) coconut milk
4 tablespoons Tamarind
water (see page 40)
150 ml (5 fl oz) water
5 mild green finger chillies,
halved, seeded and cut into
long thin shreds
2 tablespoons chopped
coriander
Salt**

**1** To prepare the raw prawns, twist the head away from the body and discard or use for stock. Break open the soft shell along the belly and carefully peel it away from the flesh, leaving the last tail segment of the shell in place. With some large prawns you may need to remove the intestinal tract, which looks like a dark vein running down the back of the prawn flesh. Run the tip of a small knife down the back of the prawn to expose the gut and then pull it away.

**2** Mix the prawns with the vinegar and ½ teaspoon of salt and leave for 5 minutes or so. This enhances the flavour. Meanwhile, put the turmeric powder, peppercorns, coriander seeds, cumin seeds and white poppy seeds, if using, into a spice grinder and grind to a fine powder.

**3** Heat the oil in a medium-sized pan. Add the onion, garlic and ginger and fry gently for 5 minutes. Stir in the ground spices and fry for 2 minutes. Add the ground almonds if you aren't using poppy seeds, plus the coconut milk, tamarind water, water, three-quarters of the sliced chillies and ½ teaspoon of salt. Bring to a simmer and cook for 5 minutes. Add the prawns and simmer for only 3–4 minutes so they don't overcook. Stir in the rest of the sliced chillies and the chopped coriander and serve with some steamed basmati rice (see page 42).

# roast monkfish with crushed potatoes

SERVES 4

**2 x 350 g (12 oz) pieces of thick monkfish fillet**
**750 g (1½ lb) new potatoes, scraped clean**
**2 tablespoons olive oil**
**85 ml (3 fl oz) extra virgin olive oil, plus extra to serve**
**50 g (2 oz) watercress sprigs, very roughly chopped**
**Balsamic vinegar, sea salt flakes and coarsely crushed black pepper, to serve**

**1** Preheat the oven to 200°C/400°F/Gas Mark 6. Season the monkfish with some salt and set it aside for 15 minutes.

**2** Cook the potatoes in well-salted boiling water until tender. While the potatoes are cooking, heat the 2 tablespoons of olive oil in a large, ovenproof frying pan. Pat the monkfish dry on kitchen paper, add to the pan and sear for 3–4 minutes, turning it 3 or 4 times, until nicely browned on all sides. Transfer the pan to the oven and roast for 10–12 minutes, until the fish is cooked through but still moist and juicy in the centre. Remove from the oven, cover with foil and set aside for 5 minutes.

**3** When the potatoes are done, drain them well and return them to the pan with the extra virgin olive oil. Gently crush each potato against the side of the pan with the back of a fork until it just bursts open. Season with salt and pepper, add any juices from the fish and the watercress and turn over gently until the watercress is well mixed in.

**4** Cut the monkfish across into thick slices. Spoon the crushed potatoes on to 4 warmed plates and put the monkfish on top. Put your thumb over the top of the bottle of extra virgin olive oil and drizzle a little of it around the outside edge of each plate. Do the same with the balsamic vinegar and then sprinkle around a few sea salt flakes and coarsely crushed black pepper.

SERVES 4

1 tablespoon caster sugar
4 tablespoons Cabernet
Sauvignon vinegar
5 tablespoons extra
virgin olive oil
4 teaspoons lemon juice
1 x 550 g (1¼ lb) piece of
unskinned wild (or
best-quality farmed)
salmon fillet, taken from
a large fish
A small bunch of basil
Salt and black pepper

1 Put the sugar into a small saucepan and leave over a low heat until it has turned into a light brown caramel – about the colour of golden syrup. Immediately remove from the heat, add the vinegar, then return to a low heat and stir with a wooden spoon until all the caramel has dissolved. Bring to the boil and reduce to 1½ tablespoons, leave to cool a little and then stir in 4 tablespoons of the oil, the lemon juice, ½ teaspoon of salt and 5 turns of the black pepper mill. Keep warm.

2 Put the salmon skin-side down on a board and, using a long, thin-bladed knife, cut at a 45-degree angle down towards the skin into 12 slices 5 mm (¼ in) thick . Brush them on both sides with the remaining oil and season lightly with salt and quite generously with black pepper.

3 Heat a ridged cast-iron griddle until smoking hot. Cook the escalopes, no more than 2 at a time, for 15 seconds on each side, turning them with a palette knife, then quickly lifting them on to a warmed baking tray.

4 Slightly overlap 3 of the salmon slices on each warmed plate. Very finely shred the basil leaves and sprinkle them around the outside edge of the plate. Spoon the warm dressing over the shredded basil. You can, if you like, garnish the salmon with some deep-fried basil leaves – just drop them into hot oil for a few seconds and then drain.

# leek cannelloni with lemon thyme

SERVES 4

1 quantity Cheese sauce
(see page 39)
50 g (2 oz) butter
900 g (2 lb) leeks, cleaned
and thinly sliced
2 garlic cloves, crushed
2 teaspoons lemon
thyme leaves
2 tablespoons water
250 g (9 oz) ricotta cheese
250 g (9 oz) fresh lasagne
pasta (12 sheets)
75 g (3 oz) provolone piccante
cheese, coarsely grated
Salt and black pepper

FOR THE TOMATO SAUCE
2 tablespoons olive oil
1 medium onion,
finely chopped
1 garlic clove, crushed
400 g (14 oz) can
chopped tomatoes
50 ml (2 fl oz) red
wine vinegar
2 teaspoons caster sugar

1 Start the cheese sauce and set aside for 20 minutes to infuse.

2 For the tomato sauce, heat the oil in a medium-sized pan. Add the onion and garlic and cook gently until softened. Add the tomatoes and simmer for 15–20 minutes, stirring now and then, until reduced and thickened. Put the vinegar and sugar into a small pan and boil rapidly until reduced to 1 teaspoon. Stir into the tomato sauce with some salt and pepper, then spoon over the base of a large, shallow ovenproof dish.

3 For the cannelloni filling, melt the butter in a large pan. Add the leeks, garlic, lemon thyme leaves and water and cook gently, uncovered, for 15 minutes, until they are tender and all the excess liquid has evaporated. Leave to cool, then beat in the ricotta and season to taste.

4 Bring a large pan of salted water to the boil. Drop in the lasagne sheets one at a time, take the pan off the heat and leave to soak for 5 minutes. Drain well and leave to cool. Spoon some leek filling along one short edge of each sheet, roll up and arrange, seam-side down, on top of the tomato sauce.

5 Preheat the oven to 200°C/400°F/Gas Mark 6. Finish making the cheese sauce. Pour over the cannelloni, sprinkle over the provolone and bake in the oven for 30 minutes until golden and bubbling.

SERVES 6

1 x 2.5 kg (5½ lb) leg of lamb
Olive oil chips (see page 41)
and Tomato, shallot and basil
salad (see page 42), to serve

FOR THE MARINADE
2 large garlic cloves, chopped
1 medium-hot Dutch red chilli,
seeded and finely chopped
1 teaspoon chopped rosemary
The leaves from 6
sprigs of thyme
1 fresh bay leaf,
finely chopped
3 strips of pared lemon zest
Juice of ½ lemon
1 teaspoon Maldon salt
½ teaspoon black pepper,
coarsely crushed
6 tablespoons olive oil

**1** To butterfly the leg of lamb, find the place where the long bone running down the length of the leg appears to be close to the surface. Split open the meat along this bone and cut it away from either side. At the fatter end of the leg there is a group of smaller bones. Continue to cut the meat away from these until you have completely opened up the leg and can lift them all out. You should now have a piece of meat shaped like butterfly wings. Trim off any excess fat and open up any thicker areas of the meat so that it is all about 4–5 cm (1½–2 in) thick. If in doubt, get your butcher to do it.

**2** For the marinade, mix the ingredients together in a shallow roasting tin. Add the lamb, turn it until well coated, then turn skin-side up, cover and leave in the fridge for at least an hour.

**3** If you are using a charcoal barbecue, light it 40 minutes before you want to start cooking. If you are using a gas barbecue, light it 10 minutes beforehand. Place the lamb on the bars of the barbecue and keep turning it, moving it to different parts of the grill if the fat starts to flare up, and cook for 10–12 minutes on each side. Alternatively, just barbecue the leg for 5–7 minutes on each side until well-coloured, then transfer it to a hot oven for 20–25 minutes.

**5** Lift the lamb on to a board, cover with foil and leave to rest for 5 minutes. Then carve into slices and serve with the chips and salad.

SERVES 4-6

1 x 1.5 kg (3 lb) piece of thick
belly pork with the rind
1 tablespoon Sichuan
peppercorns
1 teaspoon black peppercorns
2 tablespoons Maldon
sea salt flakes
2 teaspoons five-spice powder
2 teaspoons caster sugar
1 quantity Steamed Chinese
greens in oyster sauce
(see page 42) and Steamed
rice (see page 42), to serve

**1** Spike the skin of the pork with a skewer as many times as you can, going through into the fat but not so deep that you go into the flesh. Pour a kettleful of hot water over the skin, leave it to drain and then dry it off well.

**2** Heat a dry, heavy-based frying pan over a high heat. Add the Sichuan and black peppercorns and shake them around for a few seconds until they darken slightly and start to smell aromatic. Transfer to a spice grinder and grind to a fine powder. Tip into a bowl and stir in the sea salt, five-spice powder and sugar. Turn the pork flesh-side up on a tray and rub the flesh all over with the spice mixture. Set aside somewhere cool for 8 hours or overnight.

**3** Preheat the oven to 200°C/400°F/Gas Mark 6. Turn the pork skin-side up and place on a rack resting on top of a roasting tin of water. Roast for 15 minutes, then lower the oven temperature to 180°C/350°F/Gas Mark 4 and roast for a further 2 hours, topping up the water in the roasting tin when necessary.

**4** Increase the oven temperature once more to 230°C/450°F/Gas Mark 8 and continue to roast the pork for a further 15 minutes. Then remove from the oven and leave it to cool. It is best served warm. Cut the pork into bite-sized pieces and arrange on a warmed platter. Serve with the Chinese greens in oyster sauce and steamed rice.

## chicken stock

MAKES ABOUT 1.75 LITRES (3 PINTS)
**Bones from a 1.5 kg (3 lb) uncooked chicken
  or 450 g (1 lb) chicken wings
1 large carrot, chopped
2 celery sticks, sliced
2 leeks, sliced
2 fresh or dried bay leaves
2 sprigs of thyme
2.25 litres (4 pints) water**

**1** Put all the ingredients into a large pan and bring just to the boil, skimming off any scum from the surface as it appears. Leave to simmer very gently for 2 hours – it is important not to let it boil as this will force the fat from even the leanest chicken and make the stock cloudy.

**2** Strain the stock through a muslin-lined sieve and use as required. If not using immediately, leave to cool, then chill and refrigerate or freeze for later use.

## fish stock (fumet)

MAKES ABOUT 1.2 LITRES (2 PINTS)
**1 kg (2¼ lb) flat-fish bones, such as lemon
  sole, brill and plaice
2.25 litres (4 pints) water
1 onion, chopped
1 fennel bulb, chopped
100 g (4 oz) celery, sliced
100 g (4 oz) carrot, chopped
25 g (1 oz) button mushrooms, sliced
1 sprig of thyme**

**1** Put the fish bones and water into a large pan, bring just to the boil and simmer very gently for 20 minutes. Strain through a sieve into a clean pan, add the vegetables and thyme and bring back to the boil. Simmer for 35 minutes or until reduced to about 1.2 litres (2 pints).

**2** Strain once more and use as required. If not using immediately, leave to cool, then chill and refrigerate or freeze for later use.

## beef broth

MAKES ABOUT 2.5 LITRES (4½ PINTS)
900 g (2 lb) shin of beef
2 celery sticks
2 carrots
2 onions
50 g (2 oz) piece of Parmesan cheese rind
   (optional)
5 litres (9 pints) water
2 bay leaves
2 sprigs of thyme
1 tablespoon salt

Put all the ingredients except the herbs and salt into a large saucepan and bring to the boil, skimming off any scum as it rises to the surface. Reduce the heat and leave to simmer for 2½ hours, adding the salt and herbs 15 minutes before the end.

## cheese sauce

MAKES ABOUT 600 ML (1 PINT)
1 small onion, peeled and halved
3 cloves
450 ml (15 fl oz) full-cream milk
1 bay leaf
½ teaspoon black peppercorns
30 g (1¼ oz) butter
30 g (1¼ oz) plain flour
2 tablespoons double cream
75 g (3 oz) provolone piccante cheese, grated
1 egg yolk

**1** Stud the onion with the cloves and put it into a pan with the milk, bay leaf and black peppercorns. Bring the milk to the boil and set aside for 20 minutes to infuse.

**2** Strain the milk. Melt the butter in a pan, add the flour and cook over a medium heat for 1 minute. Gradually beat in the milk, bring to the boil and leave to simmer over a low heat for 10 minutes, giving it a stir every now and then. Remove the pan from the heat and stir in the cream, the grated provolone, the egg yolk and some seasoning.

## mayonnaise

This recipe includes instructions for making mayonnaise in a liquidizer or by hand. It is lighter when made mechanically, because the process uses a whole egg, whereas hand-made mayonnaise is softer and richer. You can use sunflower oil or olive oil, or a mixture of the two if you prefer. It will keep in the fridge for up to 1 week.

MAKES 300 ML (10 FL OZ)

**2 egg yolks or 1 egg**
**2 teaspoons white wine vinegar**
**½ teaspoon salt**
**1 tablespoon mustard (optional)**
**300 ml (10 fl oz) sunflower oil or olive oil**

TO MAKE THE MAYONNAISE BY HAND:
Make sure all the ingredients are at room temperature before you start. Put the egg yolks, vinegar, salt and mustard, if using, into a mixing bowl and then place the bowl on a cloth to stop it slipping. Using a wire whisk, lightly whisk to break the yolks, then beat the oil into the egg mixture a few drops at a time, until you have incorporated it all.

Once you have added the same volume of oil as the original mixture of egg yolks and vinegar, you can add the remainder a little more quickly.

TO MAKE THE MAYONNAISE IN A MACHINE:
Put the whole egg, vinegar, salt and mustard, if using, into a liquidizer or food processor. Turn on the machine and then slowly add the oil through the hole in the lid until you have a thick emulsion.

## tamarind water

Take a piece of tamarind pulp about the size of a tangerine and place it in a bowl with 150 ml (5 fl oz) warm water. With your fingers, work the paste into the water until it has broken down and all the seeds have been released. Now strain the slightly syrupy mixture through a fine sieve into a bowl and discard the fibrous material left in the sieve. It is now ready to use.

## chips

Maris Piper potatoes make the best chips, but all recently dug new potatoes will make good chips. If you're using over-wintered potatoes the secret is to use ones that have been delicately handled and kept at a stable temperature – about 5°C (41°F). If not, the starch in the potatoes turns into sugar and leads to dark and greasy chips caused by caramelization. If you're planning any sort of deep-fried potato for something special, it's always a good idea to fry a couple and, if they are not perfect, buy a different bag.

Peel 550 g (1¼ lb) of medium-sized potatoes. These are the shapes I like: for thin chips, cut them into 1 cm (½ in) thick slices and then lengthways into chips; for roughly cut chips, cut the potatoes into wedges; and for goose fat chips (see below), cut them into 1 cm (½ in) thick slices and then lengthways into 2 cm (¾ in) wide, flatter chips. Quickly rinse them under cold water to remove the starch and dry them well on a clean tea towel.

I like to cook most chips in groundnut oil as it is more stable at higher temperatures, but sunflower or vegetable oils are fine, too. Chips are also fantastic cooked in olive oil for certain dishes – just ordinary olive oil, not extra virgin. For goose fat chips you will need to empty about 2 x 350 g (12 oz) cans of goose fat into a medium-sized pan, so that when it has melted you have a sufficient depth in which to cook the chips – the pan should not be more than one-third full. Heat the oil or goose fat to 120°C/250°F. Drop a large handful of the chips into a chip basket and cook them in batches until they are tender when pierced with the tip of a knife, but have not taken on any colour – about 5 minutes. Lift out and drain. To finish, heat the oil or fat to 190°C/375°F and cook them in batches until crisp and golden – about 2 minutes. Lift them on to kitchen paper, drain and then sprinkle with salt. Serve immediately.

## tomato, shallot and basil salad

SERVES 4-6

Whisk together 4 tablespoons of extra virgin olive oil, 1 tablespoon of sherry vinegar, ¼ of a teaspoon of caster sugar, ½ a teaspoon of salt and some freshly ground black pepper. Thinly slice 3 beef tomatoes and lay them in a single layer over the base of a large serving plate. Sprinkle with 1 very thinly sliced shallot, the dressing and then 6-8 finely shredded basil leaves. Finish with a little more coarsely ground black pepper and serve immediately.

## steamed chinese greens in oyster sauce

SERVES 4-6

Cut 8-12 small heads of pak choi lengthways into quarters and put them on to an opened-out petal steamer. Lower them into a shallow pan containing about 1 cm (½ in) of simmering water, cover and steam for 3-4 minutes or until tender. Meanwhile, mix together 2 teaspoons of sunflower oil, 1 teaspoon of sesame oil, 4 tablespoons of oyster sauce and 1 tablespoon of dark soy sauce in a small pan and leave to warm through over a low heat. Transfer the pak choi to a warmed serving plate, spoon over the sauce and serve.

## steamed rice

SERVES 4

Rinse 350 g (12 oz) of long grain or basmati rice in cold water until the water runs relatively clear. Drain, tip into a 20 cm (8 in) heavy-based saucepan and add ½ a teaspoon of salt and 600 ml (1 pint) of boiling water. Quickly bring to the boil, stir once, cover with a tight-fitting lid and reduce the heat to low. Cook the basmati rice for 10 minutes and the long grain rice for 15 minutes. Uncover, fluff up the grains with a fork and serve.

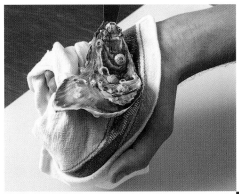

**2** Now slide the knife under the top shell to sever the ligament that joins the oyster to the shell. The ligament is slightly right of centre in the shell. Lift off the top shell, trying not to let any fragments fall on to the oyster and keeping the bottom shell upright so as not to lose any of the juice. Pick out any little pieces of shell that might have broken off into the oyster.

### opening oysters

**1** Scrub any grit off the oyster shells. Wrap one hand in a tea towel and hold the oyster in it with the bowl-shaped half of the shell underneath. Take an oyster knife or small, thick-bladed knife in your other hand. Push the point of the knife into the hinge of the oyster. Work the knife forwards and backwards to break the hinge. As the hinge breaks, twist the point of the knife to lever the top shell upwards.

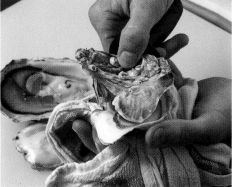

## Liquid volume measures

1 teaspoon = 5 ml

1 tablespoon (UK/US) = 3 teaspoons = 15 ml

1 tablespoon (AUS) = 4 teaspoons = 20 ml

*Note: tablespoon sizes in this book are UK/US, so Australian readers should measure 3 teaspoons where 1 tablespoon is specified in a recipe.*

2 fl oz (¼ cup) = 50 ml

4 fl oz (½ cup) = 125 ml

1 cup (8 fl oz) = 250 ml

1 US pint (16 fl oz) = 450 ml

1 UK/AUS pint (20 fl oz) = 600 ml

## Cup measures

Cup measurements, which are used by cooks in Australia and America, vary from ingredient to ingredient. You can use kitchen scales to measure solid/dry ingredients, or follow this handy selection of cup measurements for recipes in this book.

**bacon lardons, smoked/diced smoked bacon slices** 50 g (2 oz) = ¼ cup

**butter** 25 g (1 oz) = 2 tablespoons (UK/US); 50 g (2 oz) = ¼ cup; 75 g (3 oz) ⅜ cup

**carrot, chopped** 100 g (4 oz) = 1¼ cups

**celery, sliced** 100 g (4 oz) = 1¼ cups

**flour** 25 g (1 oz) = ¼ cup; 75 g (3 oz) = ¾ cup

**haricot beans** 225 g (8 oz) = 1 cup

**leeks, cleaned and sliced** 900 g (2 lb) = 4 cups

**lobster meat** 675 g (1½ lb) = 3 cups

**mushrooms, button** 25 g (1 oz) = ¼ cup; 225 g (8 oz) = 2 cups

**Parmesan cheese, grated** 15 g (½ oz) = 2 tablespoons (UK/US); 50 g (2 oz) = ½ cup

**potatoes, peeled and diced** 900 g (2 lb) = 6 cups; 1.25 kg (2½ lb) = 7½ cups

**provolone piccante cheese, grated** 150 g (5 oz) = 1¼ cups

**ricotta cheese** 250 g (9 oz) = 1 cup + 2 tablespoons

**sausage, smoked, diced** 225 g (8 oz) = 1 cup

**vegetables, assorted green, chopped** 550 g (1¼ lb) = 5 cups

**watercress, roughly chopped** 50 g (2 oz) = 2 cups

## Useful equivalents for American and Australian readers

**aubergine** eggplant

**bacon lardons** substitute diced smoked bacon slices

**beef shin** beef shank, or substitute beef soup bones

**belly pork with the rind** fresh (uncured) pork belly or side pork with the skin left on

**chervil** also known as French parsley

**chilli, green finger** fresh, green cayenne pepper; or substitute Thai pepper or jalapeño pepper

**chilli, red Dutch** also known as Holland chilli; substitute fresh, red cayenne pepper or other

**coriander (leaves)** cilantro or Chinese parsley

**cream, double (48% butterfat)** whipping or heavy cream

**cream, single (min. 18% butterfat)** light or table cream

**eggs, medium (UK/AUS)** large (US)

**flour, plain** all-purpose flour

**groundnut oil** peanut oil

**guinea fowl** substitutes include pheasant, Cornish game hen or free-range chicken

**Guinness** stout

**haricot beans** dry, white beans, also known as navy beans

**lamb, minced** ground lamb meat

**lengthways** lengthwise

**lettuce, 'hothouse'** butterhead lettuce

**Maldon sea salt flakes** sea salt (or plain salt)

**Maris Piper potatoes** white potatoes

**milk, full-cream** whole milk

**monkfish** substitutes include red snapper or lobster

**oyster sauce** if unavailable, substitute soy sauce

**pak choi** substitutes include Chinese cabbage, chard or other greens

**provolone piccante cheese** an aged, or sharp provolone; substitute mozzarella or mature Monterey Jack

**sausage, smoked** smoked, cured sausage; or substitute pepperoni or salami

**shallots** shallot onions (*not* green onions, or spring onions)

**Sichuan peppercorns** unavailable in US; substitute with Sancho Japanese peppercorns, prickly ash berries or Sichuan pepper oil

**spring onions** scallions, green onions, or (confusingly in Australia) shallots

**sugar, caster** a fine-grained sugar; substitute berry sugar or granulated sugar

**tamarind pulp** if tamarinds are unavailable, substitute limes or lemons

**tomatoes, beef** beefsteak, or slicing tomatoes

**The Seafood Restaurant**
Riverside
Padstow
Cornwall PL28 8BY

**T** 01841 532 700
**E** for table and room bookings:
reservations@rickstein.com

**St Petroc's Hotel and Bistro**
4 New Street
Padstow
Cornwall PL28 8EA

contact details as for
The Seafood Restaurant

**Rick Stein's Café**
10 Middle Street
Padstow
Cornwall PL28 8AP

contact details as for
The Seafood Restaurant

**Stein's Fish & Chips**
Waterfront Business Units
South Quay
Padstow
Cornwall PL28 8BL

contact details as for
The Seafood Restaurant

**Stein's Gift Shop**
8 Middle Street
Padstow
Cornwall PL28 8AP

**T** 01841 532 221
**F** 01841 533 566
**E** reservations@rickstein.com

Mail order:
**T** 01841 533 250
**F** 01841 533 132
**E** mailorder@rickstein.com

**Stein's Patisserie**
1 Lanadwell Street
Padstow
Cornwall PL28 8AN

contact details as for
The Seafood Restaurant

**Stein's Deli**
Waterfront Business Units
South Quay
Padstow
Cornwall PL28 8BL

contact details as for
The Seafood Restaurant

**Padstow Seafood School**
Waterfront Business Units
South Quay
Padstow
Cornwall PL28 8BL

**T** 01841 533 466
**F** 01841 533 344
**E** seafoodschool@rickstein.com

**Website** for all information:
www.rickstein.com